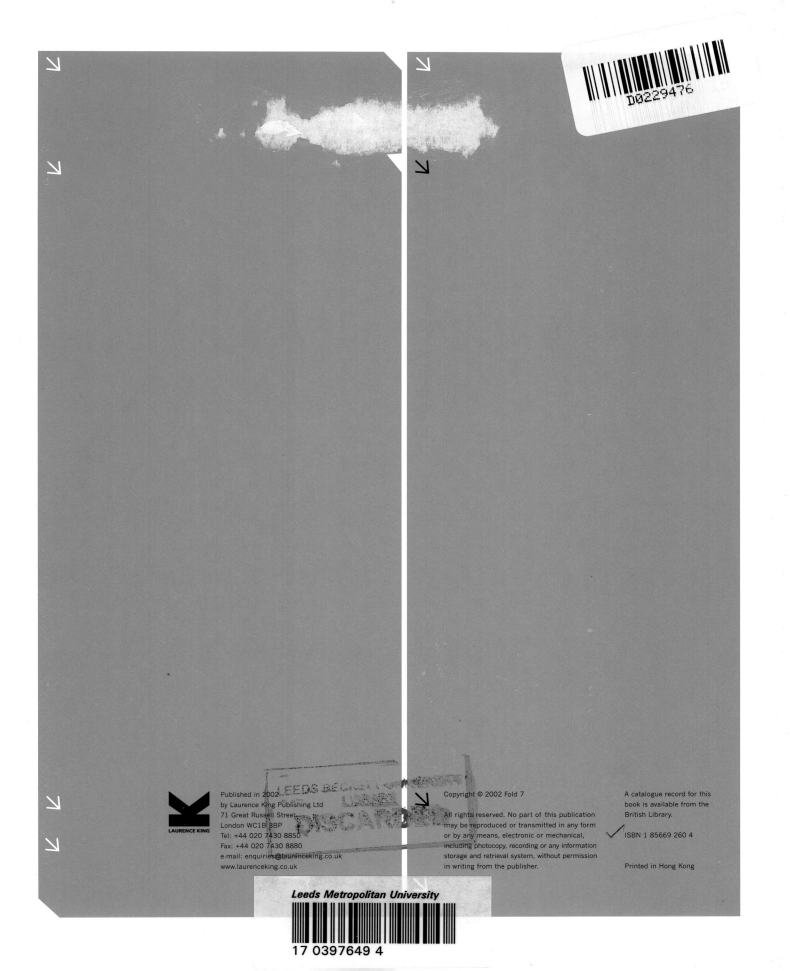

Published in 2002
by Laurence King Publishing Ltd
71 Great Russell Street,
London WC1B 3BP
Tel: +44 020 7430 8850
Fax: +44 020 7430 8880
e·mail: enquiries@laurenceking.co.uk
www.laurenceking.co.uk

A catalogue record for this
book is available from the
British Library.

ISBN 1 85669 260 4

Printed in Hong Kong

Water. A liquid. To a chemist, H_2O. Oxygen, two hydrogens. A mix of things to make other things. Two gasses make a liquid. The ingredients aren't always what you'd expect.

Have your website built by an illustrator, your pop promo written by a graffiti artist, have a photographer sign the cheques. A DJ can design the font for the record cover illustrated by the civil engineer, then we'll get the jeweller to send the invoice. School, college, exam results, it doesn't matter. Do what you're good at, do what you love. All the perfect ingredients already exist around you, everywhere you look and in everyone you meet.

You just have to learn to mix them right.

Fold7, then, are the masters of mixing, a blender among forks in the creativemarketingmediadesign world. We're always talking about those other forkin' designers, while we blend, chop, slice and dice, sauté, bake, steam and fry. You'll always see us in the kitchen at parties.

The book you hold here is a selection of experimental design created through the chain reaction of the right ingredients, their thoughts and ideas, mixed in a test tube, heated over a flame, and distilled to get the essence of Fold7.

An experiment with print. Taking it back to basics. Limiting ourselves as a test. Learning. Playing. Having fun.

We open the first section of this book with the colours Cyan, Magenta or Yellow, and the non-colour Black. Working with a palette of objects, ideas, words, thoughts. A palette consisting of the F7 logo, chemicals, cars, a photograph of a member of Fold7 staff, a diagram, a cube, and a heptagon. Introducing them one at a time, exploring them individually.

These are the ingredients, let the experiment begin.

01.1
Fold7 Logo

Logos are our friends. They give a "face" to a company, a face that's easy to recognise in a crowd. I can never remember names, but I always remember faces.

As children we learn the alphabet. We are taught to make the sounds and draw the shapes, until they are one and the same in our minds. As we grow older, become aware of different products, companies, services, we start to add their "letter", the mark that identifies them, into the alphabet in our heads. The collection of assorted letters that form the company name become replaced with an icon, we read one character instead of many.

Logos make life simpler.

01.2
Chemical

I got the poison · I got the remedy

Smoking leaves of Catnip (Nepeta Cataria) produces only mild effects in man. Freshly picked leaves are possibly more potent. Seeds seem to be readily available.

About 75 grams of Nutmeg taken in milk (25 grams per glass · skull it) will, after about 3 hours, produce some interesting effects, including visual hallucinations. The active constituents are similar to mescaline and amphetamines.

Blossoms of Canary Weed (Genista Canarien) give a mild psychedelic effect when smoked. Plants are available at many nurseries.

Club Moss (Lycopodium Gnidiodes) is said to be very similar to marijuana when smoked. Some members of the genus Myrothamnus are also active.

Known as Kava Kava, Piper Methysticum extracts have been used in Polynesia for thousands of years, and Piper Plantagiveum is similarly used in Mexico and the Caribbean. Produces a sleepy, relaxed feeling with eventual difficulty in walking. About 3 grams necessary. Grind the root into a powder; mix it into some orange juice, and drink.

Who needs chemicals?

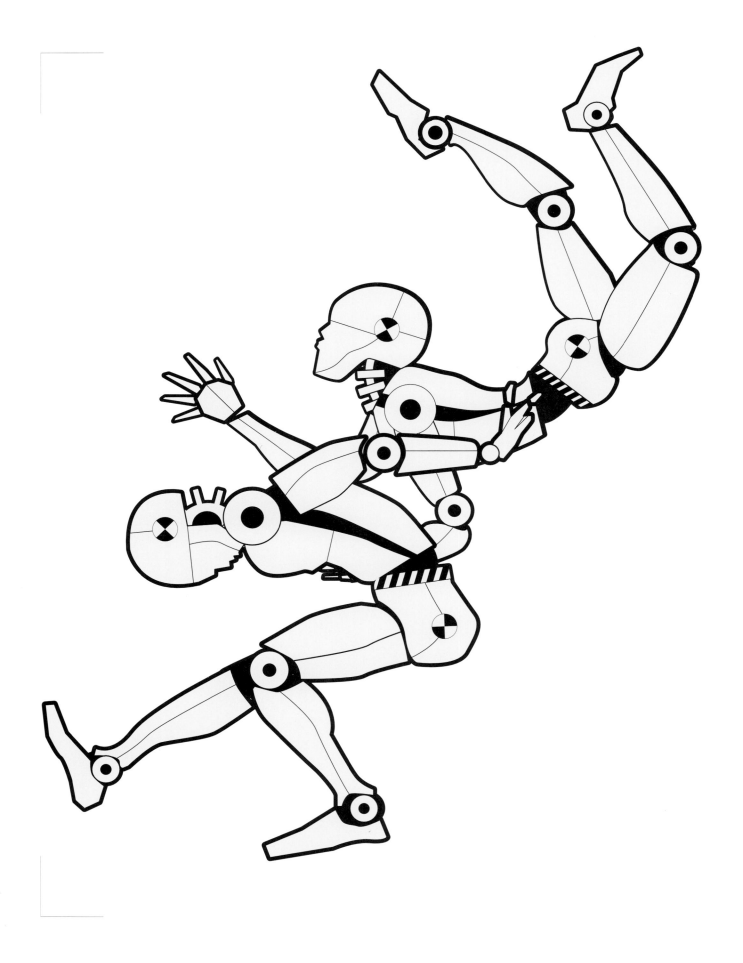

01.3 Car

Two cyclists discuss cars.

"Car. Car. What is a car?"

"A metal box on wheels."

"A coffin on wheels. As the graffiti at Twyford Downs said · Car or Planet."

"Cars suck."

"That reminds me. Nina's friend, some Swedish girl whose name I can't recall, works as a researcher for Eurotrash. She basically has to surf the web all day looking for porn, searching out people with weird sexual perversions. Anyway, she had to find guys who have sex with their cars."

"They have sex with their cars?"

"Yeah. She had to talk to this dude on the phone, ask him all about his love of upholstery and shit, find out what he does with his car. I walked out of the discussion when she started telling how he said you have to be extra careful when doing it with the exhaust pipe..."

01.4
Photograph of a member of Fold7 staff

I look at my collection of photographs of all the people I work with. My colleagues, my friends, my peers and my mentors. So many photographs, so many involving alcohol.

Ah, look at this one - Henry, looking like a gangster as he clutches two handguns across his chest. They say every picture tells a story, and this one tells a classic.

It was a few years back, and we were working on an identity and record cover for a musician who shall remain nameless. He arrived at the studio one morning for a meeting carrying a large black holdall. From the bag he produced two handguns. On seeing these, Ryan immediately turned white, made his excuses, and shut himself away at the far end of the studio. The buzzer sounded, and I answered the door to a courier, who handed me a long package, addressed to our musician friend. I signed for the package and took it to our gun-toting client.

"Your samurai swords have arrived", I joked.

"What makes you say that?" he replied, with an evil glint in his eye, as he unsheathed two ancient, but deadly looking samurai swords.

Later that day, after our client had left, Ryan told us of the dream he had had the previous night. In his dream, the client had arrived at the studio, pulled out a gun, and not unlike the scene in *The Terminator* when Arnie shoots up the police station, proceeded to gun down every

member of staff right in front of his eyes.

Yup, that photograph of Henry certainly brings back memories. But my favourite picture is of him sitting at his desk, head drooping forwards, totally asleep. Work hard, play hard, sleep hard.

DIAGRAM

At the front is a pipe, about 2.5 centimetres across, the walls of the pipe being approximately 3 millimetres thick. The inside of the pipe is grooved from end to end. The pipe protrudes 6 centimetres from a circular part which has a round ended rectangular piece sticking out at 9 o'clock. This part contains 2 small holes. The top edge of the circular part is surrounded on one side by a raised section part of the central section. This section is square with a smaller square removed from the top left corner. The top right

At the front is a pipe, about 2.5 centimetres across, the walls of the pipe being approximately 3 millimetres thick. The inside of the pipe is grooved from end to end.

The pipe protrudes 6 centimetres from a circular part, which has a round-ended rectangular piece sticking out at 9 o'clock. This part contains 2 small holes. The top edge of the circular part is surrounded on one side by a raised section, part of the central section.

↗

This section is square with a smaller square removed from the top left corner. The top right and bottom left corners have a two-sided box-shaped tube; the ends carry another section, which is shaped like a letter U with the top squeezed in. It looks like it should grip a wire or a pipe. On the left side is another section protruding as far out as the corner sections. The end is shaped to hold a pipe. The square section contains three shorter tubes, two of which are shorter, and look like they are holes for screws to attach this piece to another object.

Look, wouldn't it just be easier if I showed you a diagram?

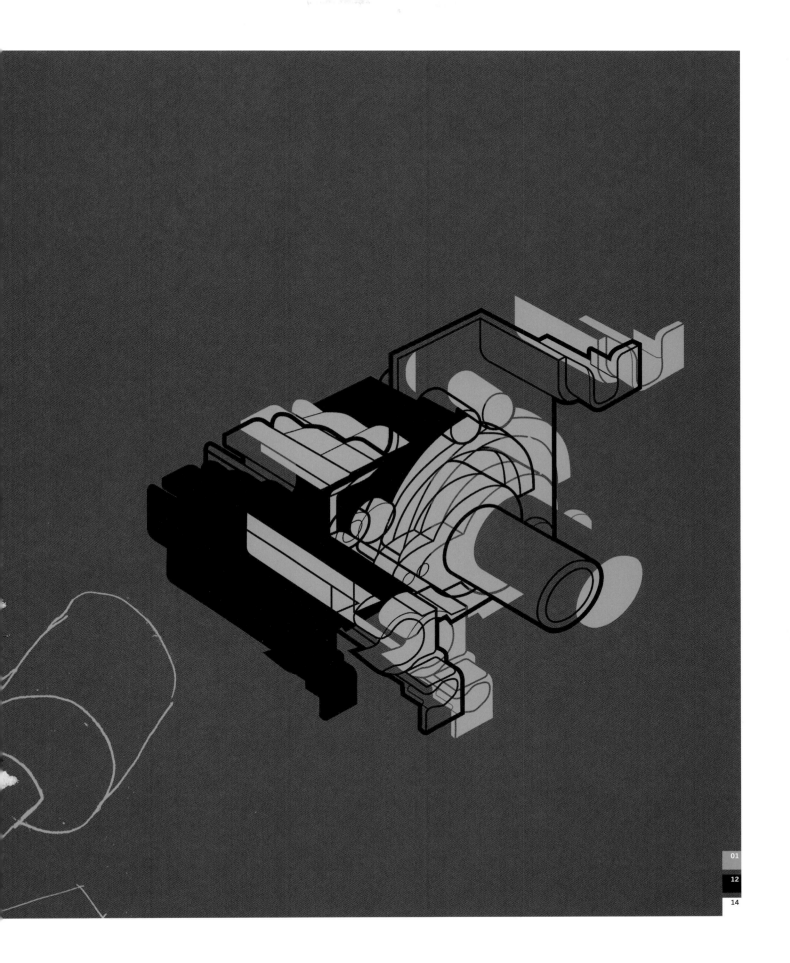

01.6 Cube

As a treat, my dad's aunt used to let us have a sugar cube from her silver sugar cube caddy. Now I think about it, that can't be true. I think we used to steal them when she wasn't looking. This aunt would never knowingly let us do something as crass as eat a sugar cube. She was extremely up-tight about dirt and mess, and I'm surprised she even let us in her house, especially when my sister went through her punk phase. For a straight-laced woman born in the 1920s, the sight of her nephew's daughter in a battered black leather jacket must have had her clutching her heart gasping "My pills. My pills". I'm sure she spent the week following our visits constantly vacuuming, desperately seeking to eradicate every last grain of mud that my sister had picked up on her DM's from smoking cigarettes in the quarry behind our school.

See what I've done? I've cunningly painted an evil portrait of my sister to cover up my admission of the theft of the sugar cubes, oh those sweet, sweet cubes.

I really wanted them for a practical joke called "The Floating Sugar Cube". The idea of the practical joke, that simple piece of shocking or confusing humour, appealed to me greatly as a child, and I had numerous books on the subject. One of them was my bible.

The illustrations were extremely stylish, with easy to follow instructional diagrams, and the joke ideas were by far the most original. It taught me how to make fake parking tickets to leave on my dad's car, how to sign paint like a professional (WET PAINT, DO NOT READ, etc.) and how to attach plastic bags inside my blazer pockets so I could pour drinks and leftover school dinner into them, then casually stroll away, leaving my peers shocked, stunned, and seeing me as a god of giggles.

I was already a connoisseur of the "fly in sugar cube", and my favourite victim for this gag was my father. He would come home from work, smelling of the warmth inside his car and feeling like a solid, strong block of a man to my hugging child-sized arms.

He would sit in his favourite chair with the newspaper and his pipe, and my mother would make him a cup of tea. I would slowly and carefully carry this in from the kitchen, using that time to add my special treats, then sit squirming in the corner, waiting for the plastic bugs to break free of their sugary coffin and float to the surface. Mostly, my father wouldn't notice, and eventually I'd have to pretend to look out of the window next to his chair, and suddenly exclaim: "Ugh! What is that floating in your tea? It looks like maggots!"

"The Floating Sugar Cube" joke was much simpler. All you had to do was carefully drop sugar cubes into the tea so they stacked on top of each other, eventually looking like the top one was floating.

Simple you may think, but despite constant badgering, my mother would never buy sugar cubes. So I stole them from my great aunt. Unfortunately, the drive home was always too long for a young boy with sugar cubes in his pocket, and so I've never tried "The Floating Sugar Cube" gag.

Let me know if it works.

EXPEDITION
STAGE 1

TRANSMISSION
× 100000

"What am I going to write about heptagons?"

"Maybe it would be quite interesting to write something pretty emotional about a heptagon, for me it seems like, it really doesn't make much sense, it doesn't seem very useful. It's like some mathematical abstract."

"I wonder if heptagons ever appear in nature?"
"Maybe in snowflakes..."
"Hmmm..."

"I think we should export all our heptagons to outer space. Maybe someone else can find a use for them."

"Calling People of the Universe - Do You Need Heptagons?"

"Can you tell us what to do with this. We think it's rubbish."

"We shaped a few coins like it to give it something to do, but basically, it's useless. There's an E.U. Heptagon Mountain, we can't get rid of them."

"I think, design-wise, they look like faulty hexagons. When I draw it, it doesn't look right. It looks like..."

"An uptight circle! It's useless, what's its use? I wish I had my 'Johnny Ball Think Box' book still. He could teach me to make a pop-up, 3-D heptagon. That book was dope."

"It all starts with a line. You could say it starts with a dot... Then you have a line, then two, then a... uh..."

"Triangle."

"Triangle! Then we got a square, then a pentagon. Then we got the six one, a hexagon. They all look OK, the line, the triangle, the square and so on. Then all of a sudden we have this odd shape. Why is it there? The next one is OK, the octagon. Then nine sides, well that's basically a circle already, everything after that is just bullshit. Unless it's really big. Everything after an octagon is just a fake circle."
"But wait. A heptagon is below an octagon, and it's still just... shit."
"It's the black sheep."
"It's the black sheep of the..."
"The Gons. The Gon Family."
"So, the heptagon is the black sheep of the Gon family... I still don't know what to write about heptagons."

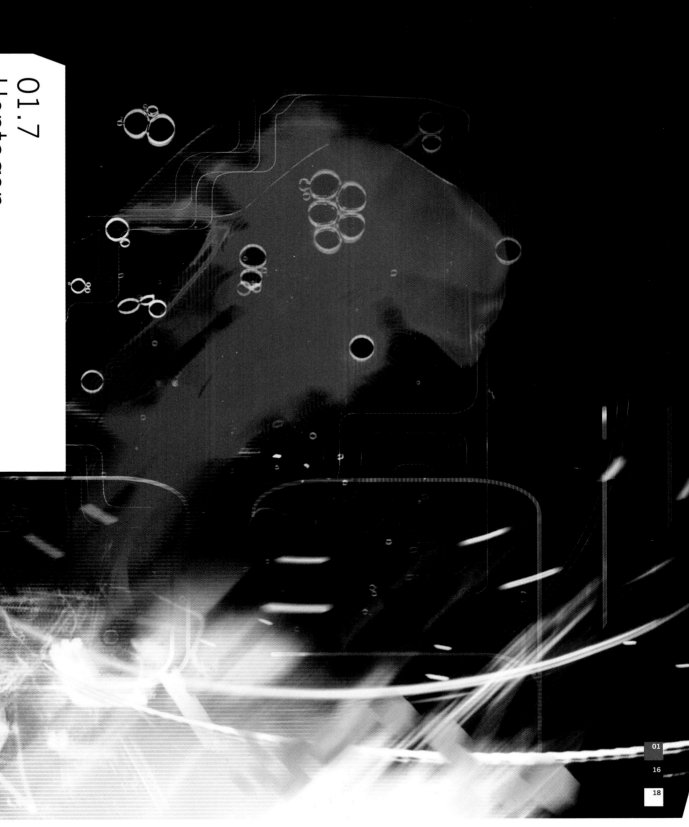

01.7
Heptagon

Initial tests show this could be interesting. Ideas, flow, pass
it on, re-mix, rewind selectah. Research subjects react well
to the objects and colours placed before them. I wonder
how those reading this report will react to our chosen
palette, and whether this reaction will be due to their
experiences, their sex, race, culture, religion? How are you
reacting? Ah, no matter, there is time for self-analysis later.

For now, the experiment continues.

3 of the process colours, 3 items from the palette. More
rules? More freedom? Turn up the heat. Increase the pressure.
Always remember to wear safety goggles...

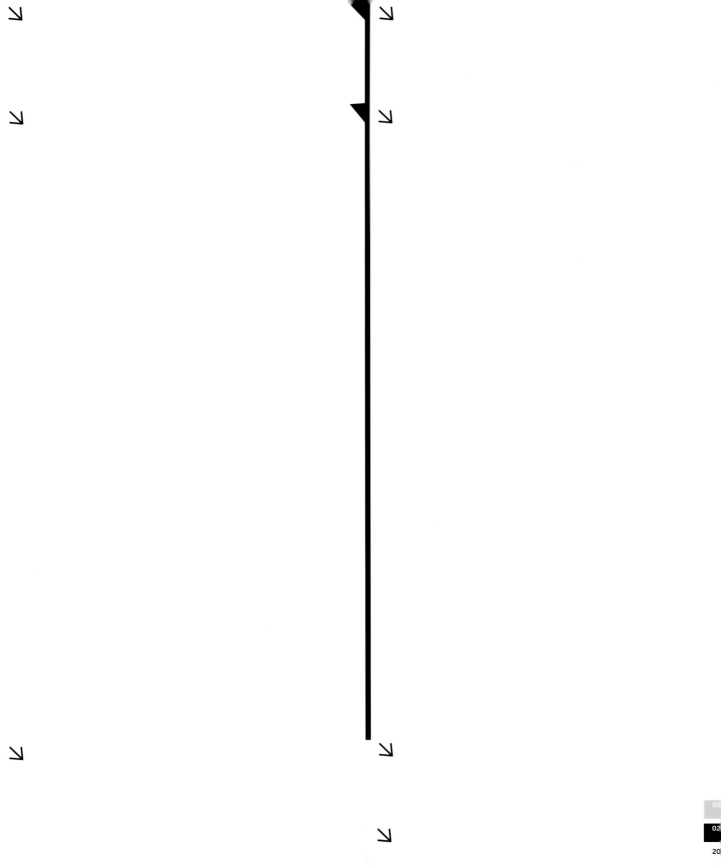

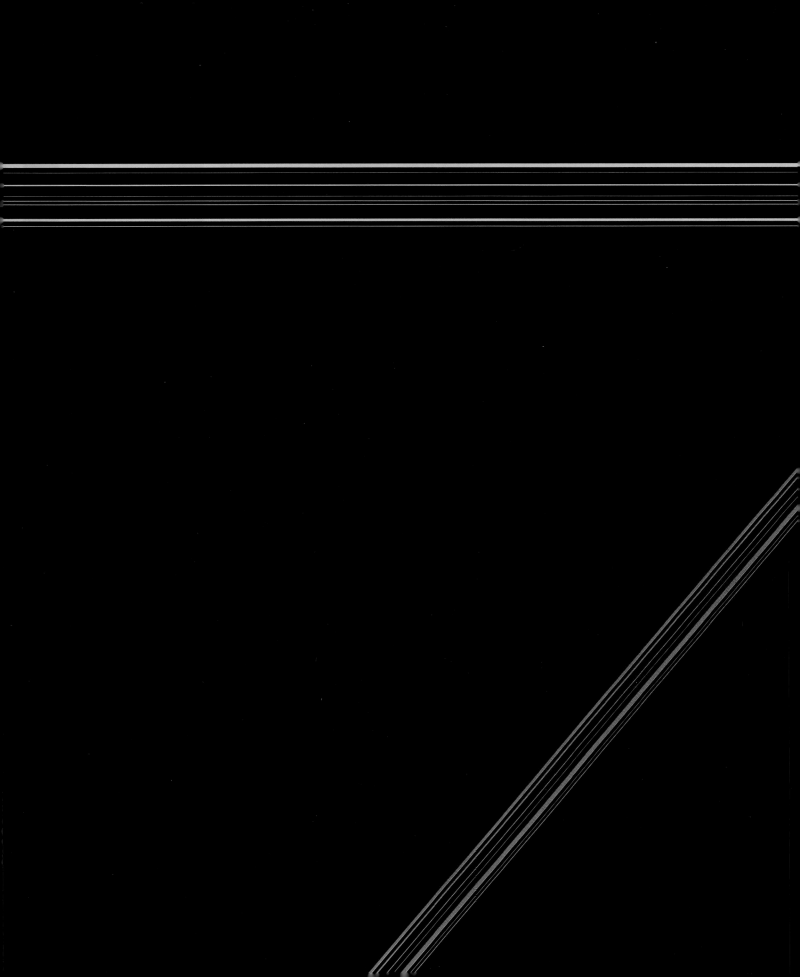

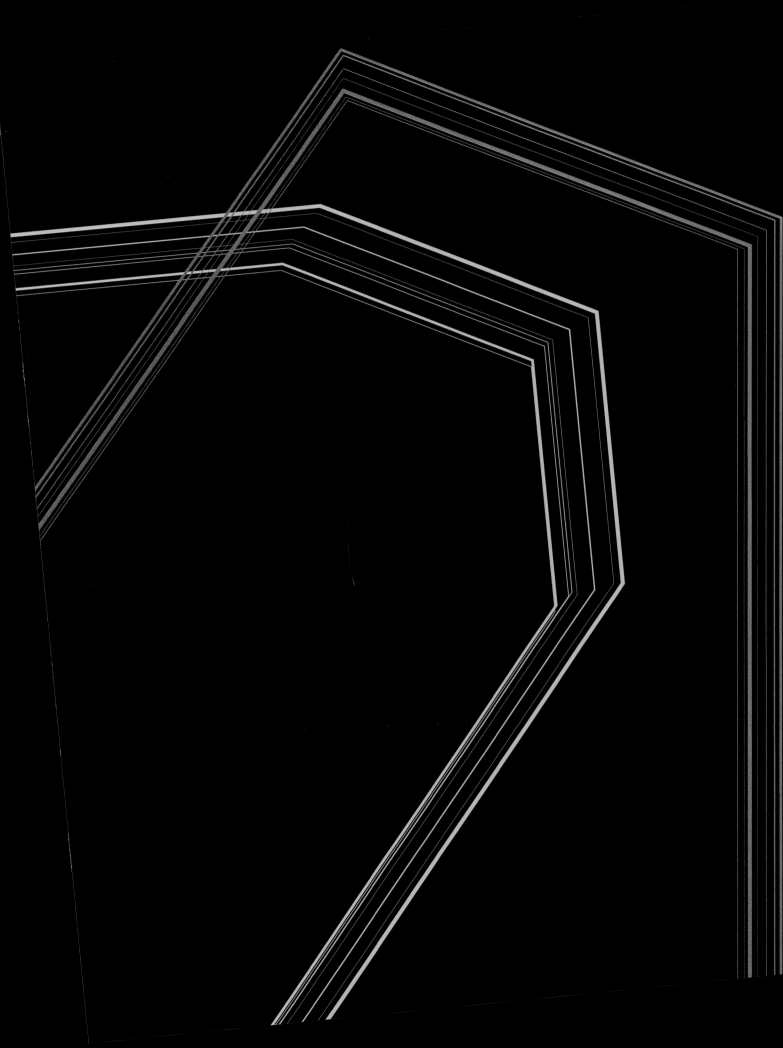

abcdefghijklmnopqrstuvwxyz

abcdefghijklmnopqrstuvwxyz

abcdefghijklmnopqrstuvwxyz
ABCDEFGHIJKLMNOPQRSTUVWXYZ

Chem

transport from the Speed

Hypothermia occurs when more heat is lost from the body than the body can produce. Although it usually happens at extremely cold temperatures, it can occur even at moderate temperatures. For example, a person will have to be freezing into cold water or wearing wet clothing in cold weather to become hypothermic. Failing to wear a hat in cold weather can also lead to hypothermia, since a large amount of body heat escapes through the head.

HEAT LOSS
PRE

alcohol tends to dilate blood vessels near the skin's surface, producing a reddening and a sense of warmth. Despite the sense of warmth, though, drinking actually decreases body temperature and increases heat loss

02

08

26

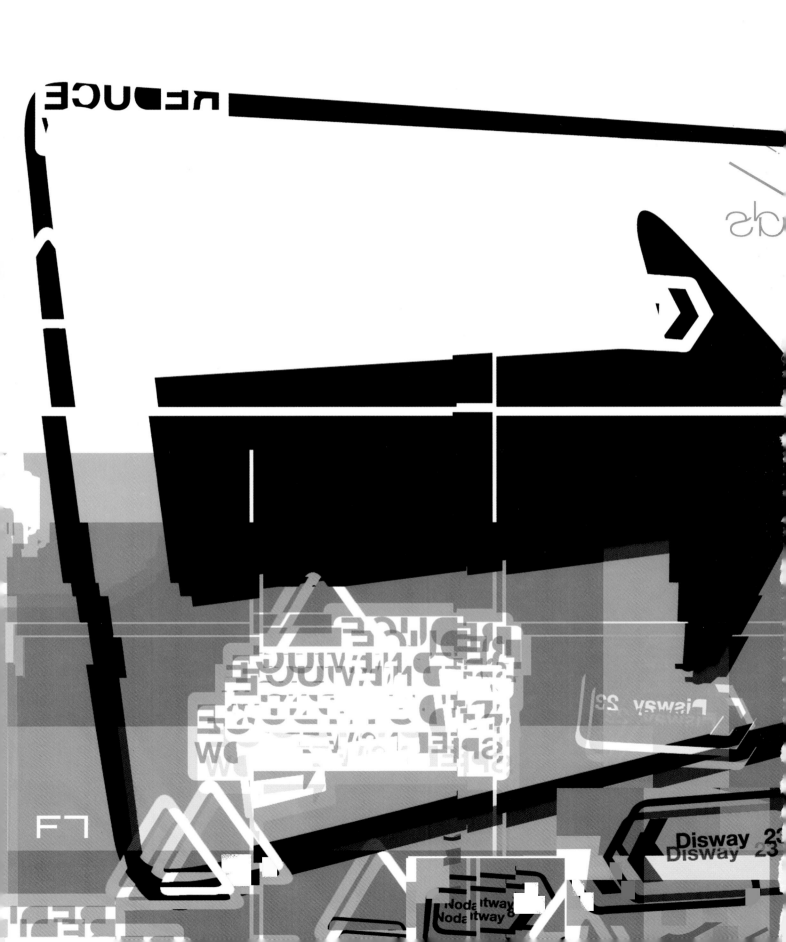

RED
SPEED

UCE
NOW

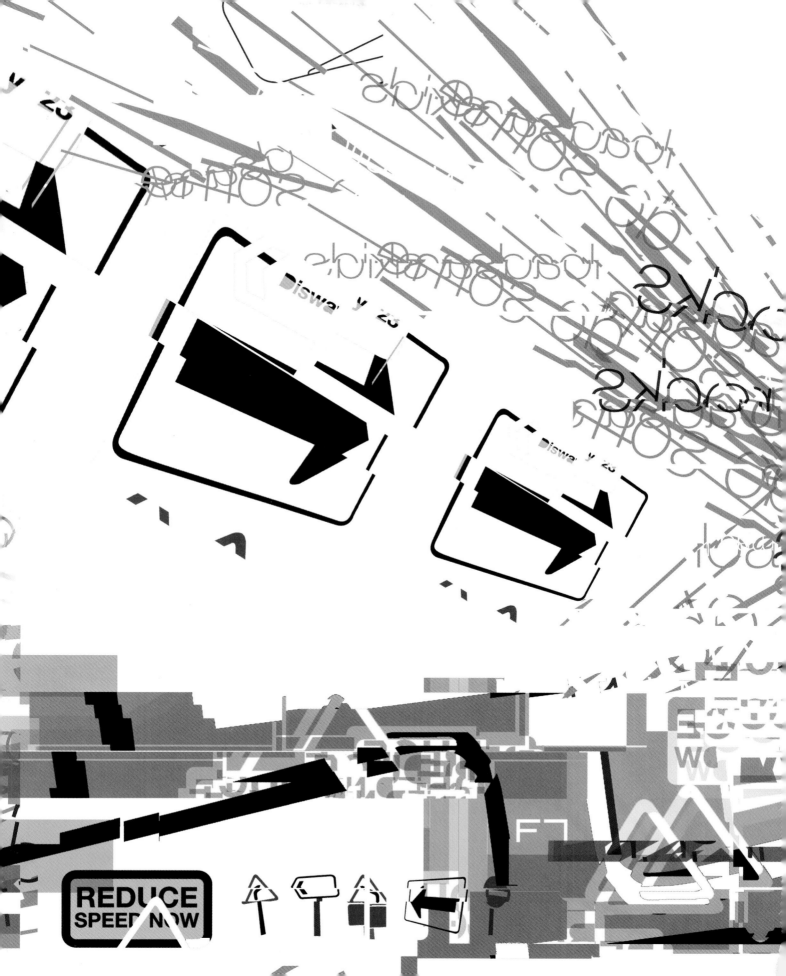

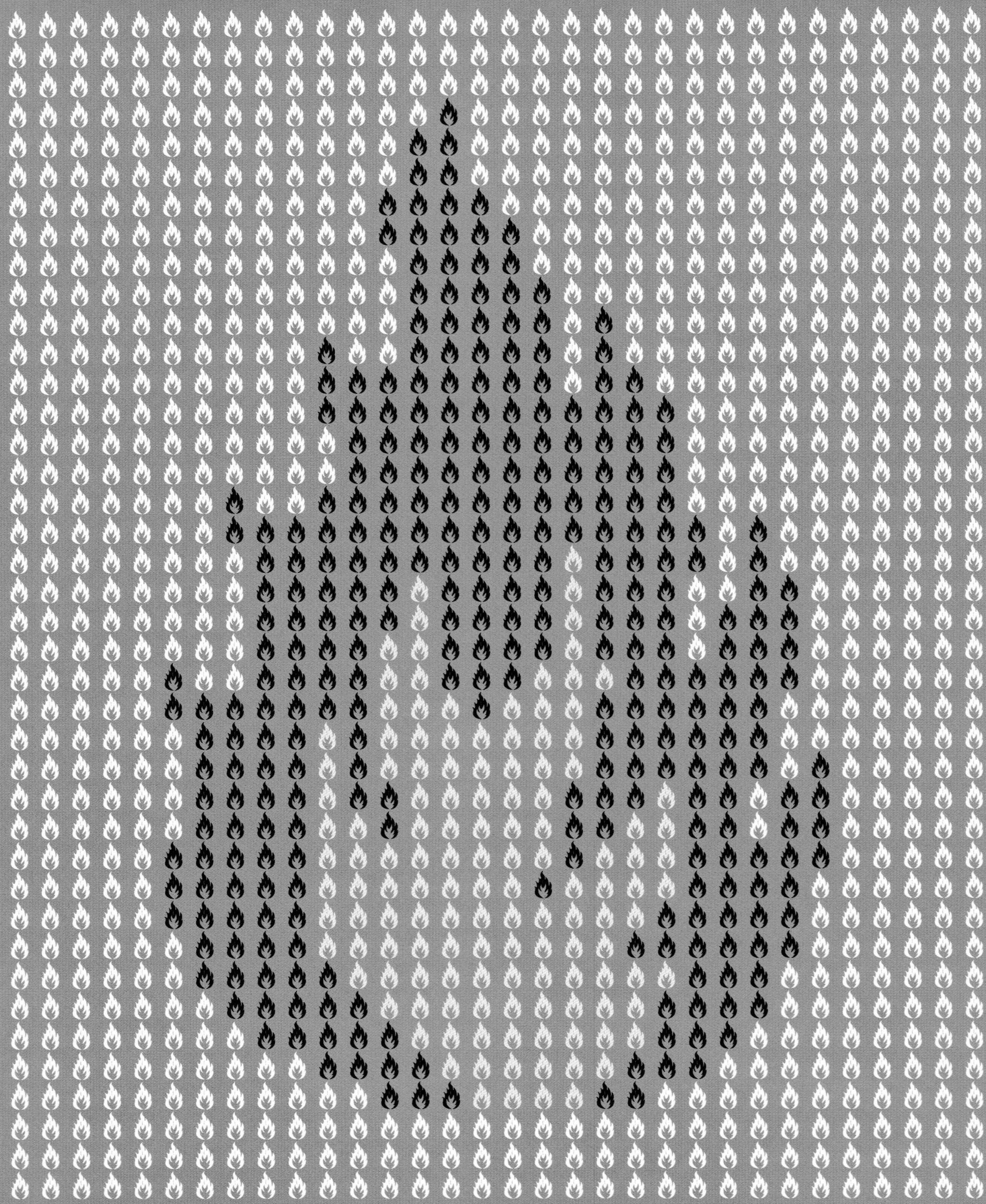

FLAMMABLE

SLEEP

RECOMMENDED DOSAGE:
8 HOURS PER EVERY 24 HOUR PERIOD

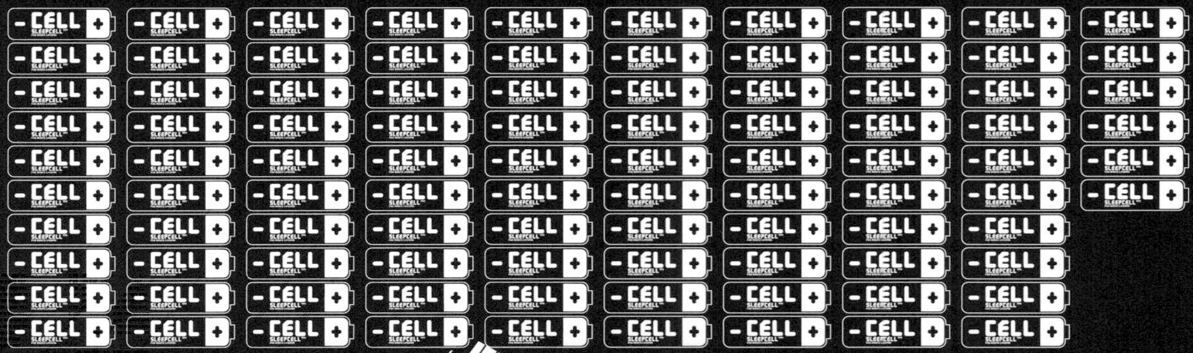

I WISH THEY WOULD HURRY UP
AND INVENT AN ANTI SLEEP PILL
[SO MUCH TO DO AND SO LITTLE TIME]

AUTOMATIC SHUTDOWN IN EFFECT!
RECHARGING VITAL SYSTEMS

[WE CAN REBUILD_]

N.S.R

Like Steve Austin on the mac,

Got Six Million Ways...

Like Steve Austin on the mic, Got Six Million Ways...

Chemistry
Introduction
Section 3

"Delicious professor. I don't understand why we don't limit our colour spectrum more often. Makes you think, what? Use the old grey stuff. And keep a tight rein on them I say. Always been one for a spot of bondage, thanks to Nanny."

It amazes me I can concentrate sometimes, surrounded by these imbeciles. Though, I must say, the old fool is right. It seems things move apace. An experiment they said, a test. And what a test they devise. Then I meet the subjects and my heart falls. This is not what I expected. Where are the black roll-neck sweaters, the thick-rimmed spectacles? Only a 17.5% shaved head ratio? Had I expected more, perhaps 80? No matter. I am a professional, a scientist. I can test anything on anyone. So let's test.

And what a test it has proven to be. My, how my children have grown. And though I could explore the effects of their solutions in this narrow, restricted field for many happy years, I have neither the time, nor the budget, to continue thus. It's time to move on once more.

Four colours now. Full colour now. Your palette, those simple building blocks to your early growth, may be put aside. Look around you, explore your surroundings, explore yourselves.

Explore.

03

SECTION ZERO 3 OF FOUR EXPERIMENTAL SECTIONS THIS SECTION HAS UNDERGONE INTENSE BOMBARDMENT WHICH MAY CAUSE PREMATURE BLINDNESS, ONLY THE BRAVE SHOULD CONSIDER ENTERING

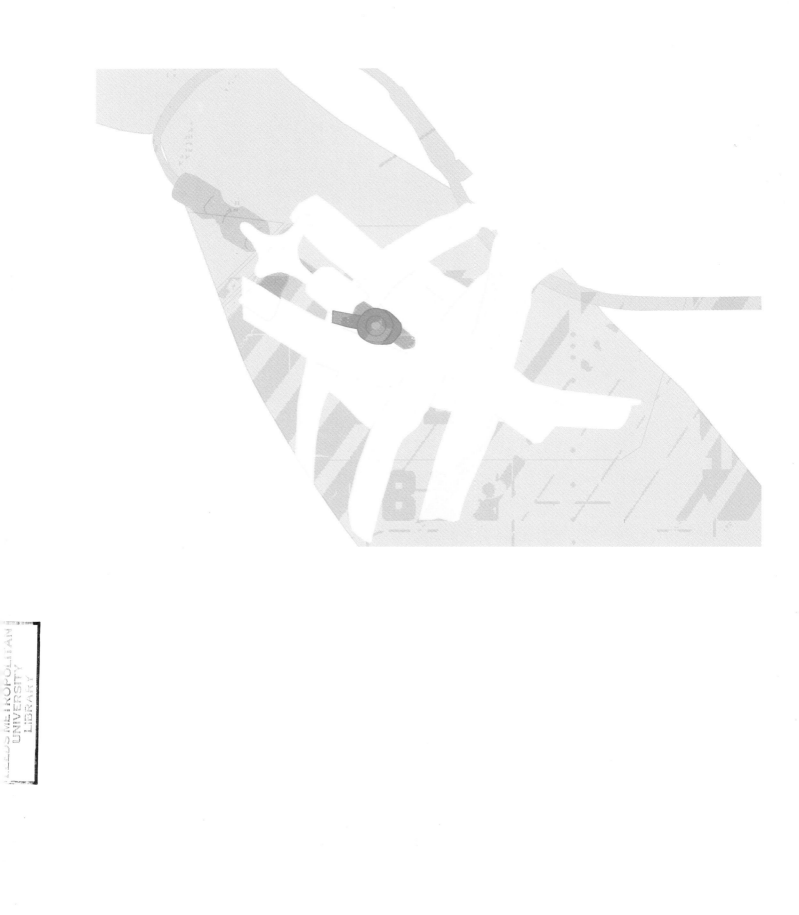

DEVELOPING
TOMORROWS
CHEMICALS

CALL
+44 (0) 207 251 0101
OR VISIT
HTTP://WWW.FOLD7.COM
TO FIND
OUT
MORE!

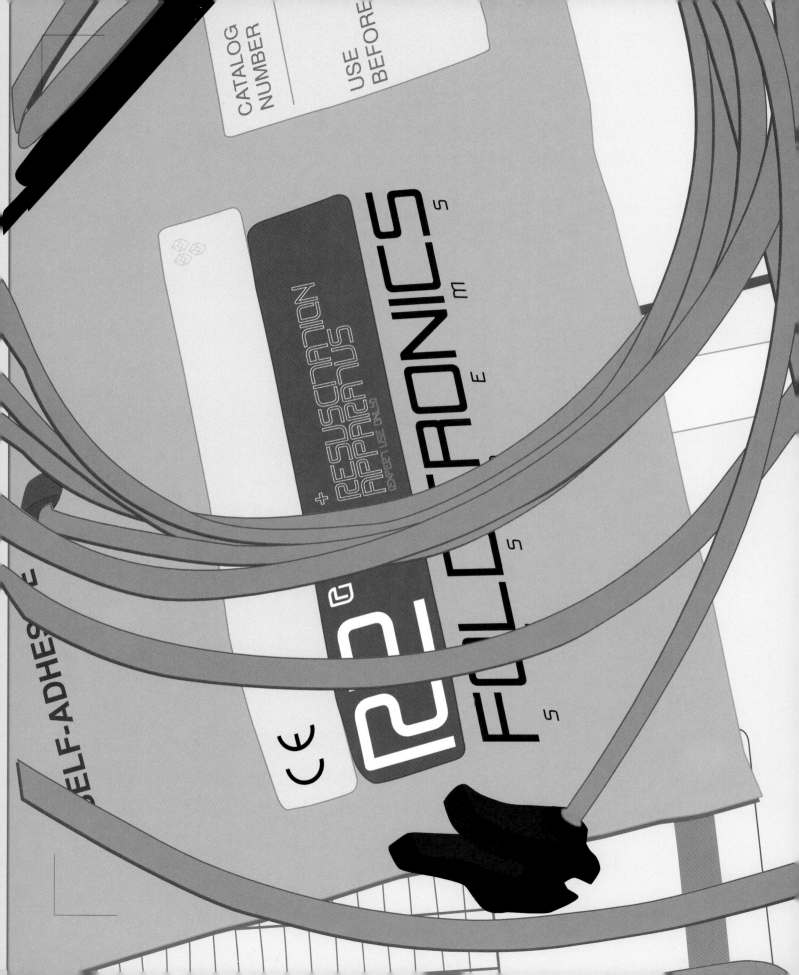

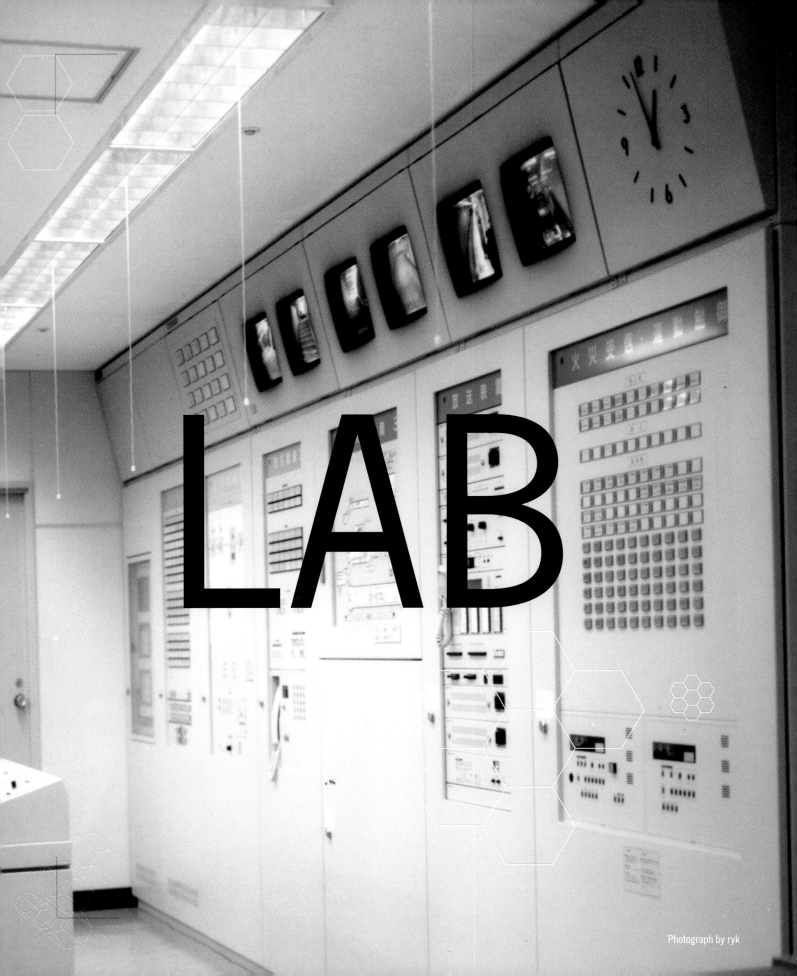

LAB

Refreshments
Staff Pantone reference chart

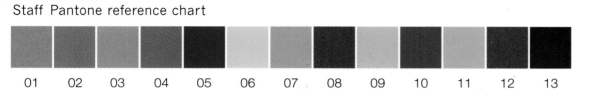

| 01 | 02 | 03 | 04 | 05 | 06 | 07 | 08 | 09 | 10 | 11 | 12 | 13 |

01 Pantone 613   Jasmine Tea
02 Pantone 172   Carrot/Ginger
03 Pantone 1385   Normal Tea (White)
04 Pantone 471   Normal Coffee (White)
05 Pantone 462   Black Coffee
06 Pantone 467   Very Milky Tea
07 Pantone 722   Light Coffee (White)
08 Pantone 724   Strong Coffee (White)
09 Pantone 466   Latte
10 Pantone 470   Strong Tea
11 Pantone 144   Light Tea (White)
12 Pantone 471   Crap Tea (White)
13 Pantone 2745   Blackcurrant Tea

IMPURE

Photograph by Guy Baker

COMPOUNDS

IMPURE COMPOUNDS:

All ideas used in dealing with solutions start, for many of us, from a base of Impure Compounds.

What are Impure Compounds? They are those sources of information that stem from the darker realms of our life. Not formulated or clean. Many do not even have relevance to what we are working on. They just exist and supply us with that visual edge that is intrinsic to our work. They could be a sound from a "messy" Jungle tune; a painful experience with a rusty needle.

01	Sx	Sex
02	Db	Dark blue
03	Ld	Line drawings
04	Tb	Tuberculosis
05	Bc	Burning cows
06	Hb	Heavy bass
07	Vg	Vector graphics
08	Mt	Melancholic tunes
09	Sd	Strange days
10	Sl	Scratchy lines
11	Ho	Heart operations

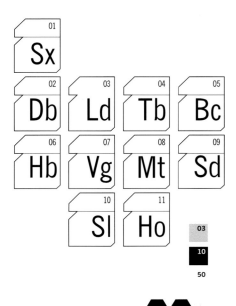

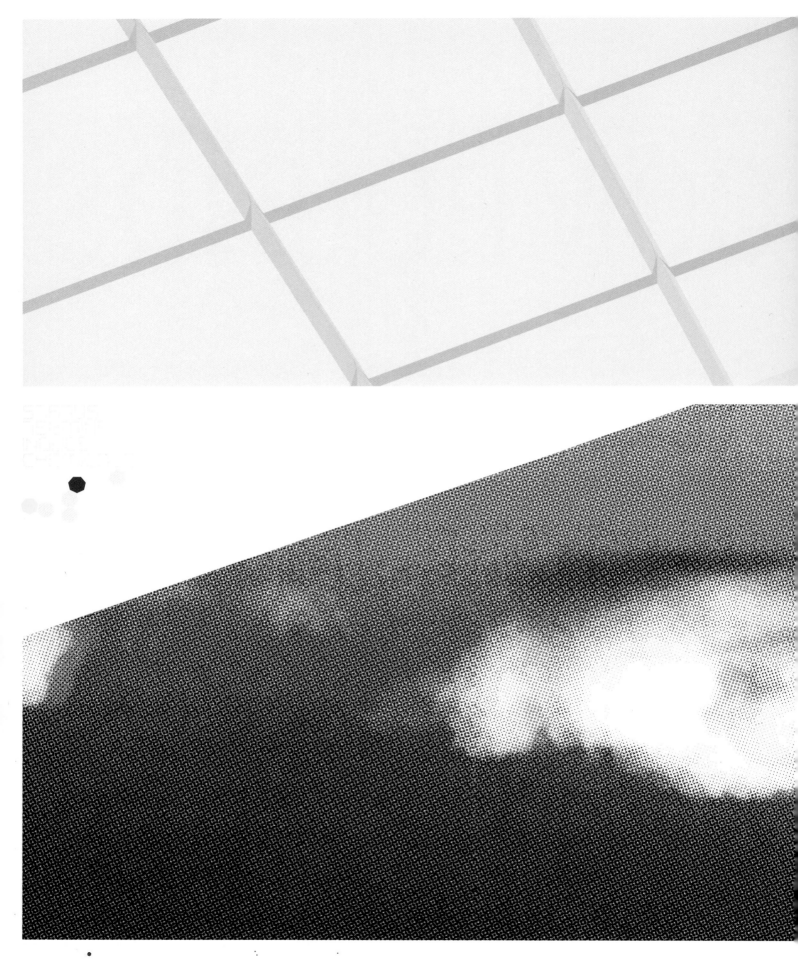

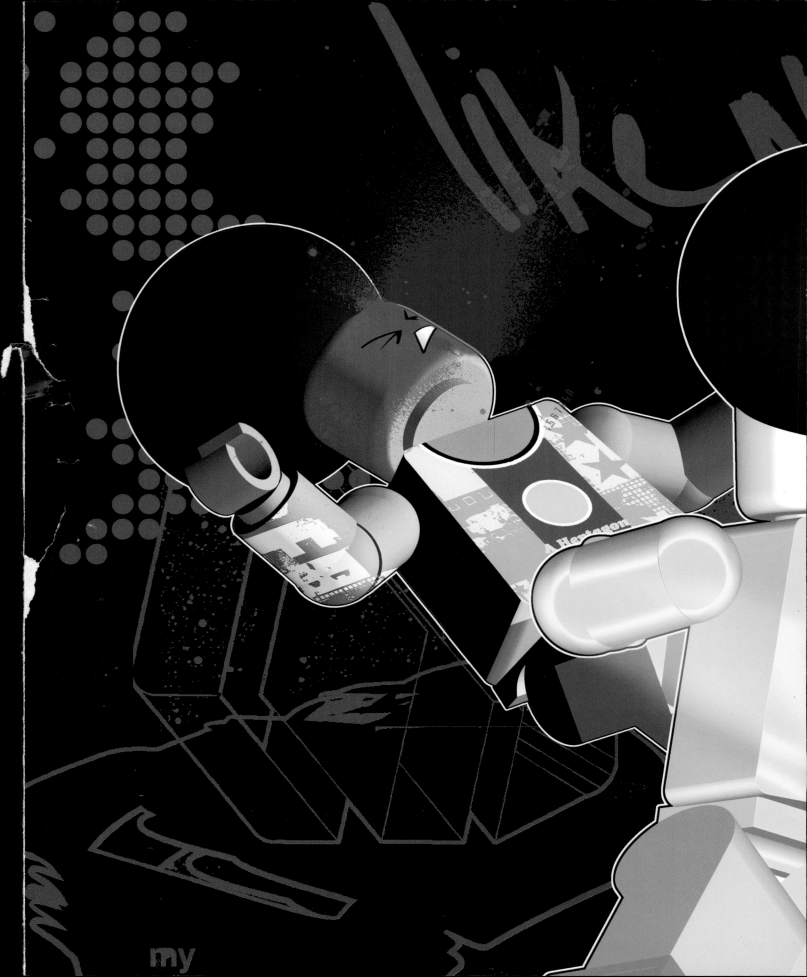

03
20
60

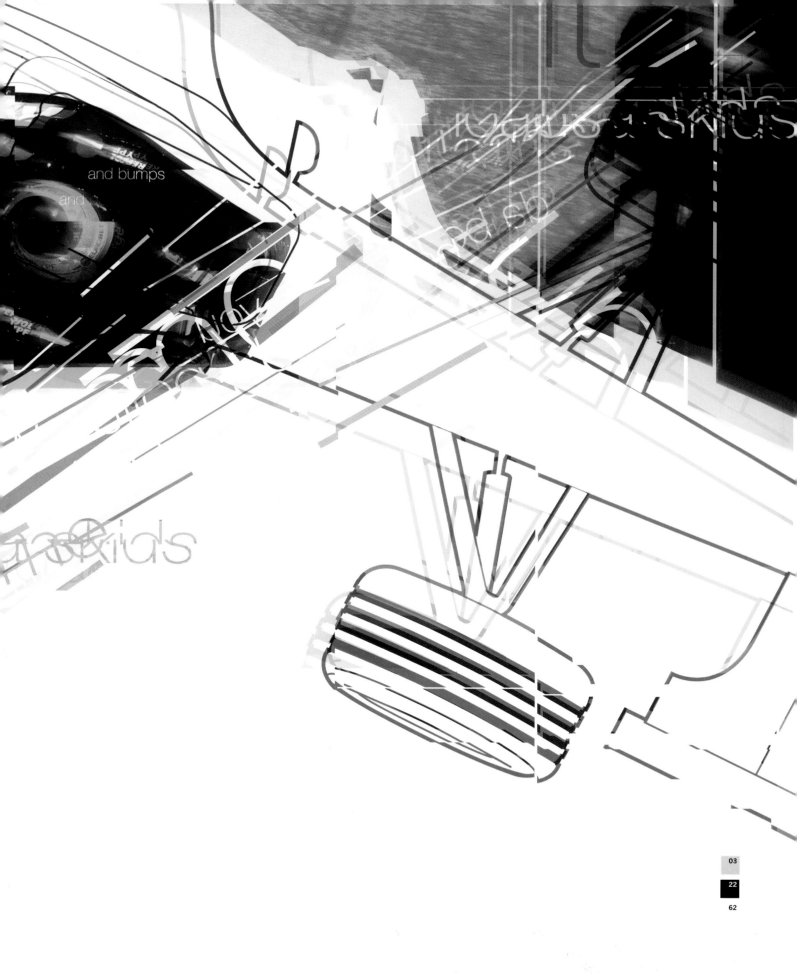

and bumps

and

"Tired, Dr. Phillpott?"

"Oh, uh, sorry Professor Anzee. Zoning. I've been here since breakfast."

"The usual toast-fest? They are strange."

"I put a banana in the enclosure as well. The big one made a play for it, as I'd expected, but then he handed it to the group's Alpha Male."

"Nothing unusual there doctor."

"Not so far, but the Alpha Male then handed it to one of the females."

"Ah, I see. Some sort of mating ritual!"

"Er. No sir. She made banana sandwiches with it. They all ate."

"How interesting. I wonder... but no, no time for this Phillpott, we're getting sidelined. Colour, Form, Typography - these are the matters at hand."

"Uh. Yes sir."

"Well? Are we ready?"

"Sir."

"Begin feed, all four units, yesterday's levels."

"Yes sir."

"Steady Miss Alberto?"

"Steady sir."

"Uh. Colour breakdown 24 parts per 100 sir."

"It'll come down. Compensate."

"Yes sir."

"Steady."

"How's the Visual Intake? Any increased brain activity?"

"Both up on yesterday's levels, and that's yesterday's peak levels sir."

"Wonderful. Must be the banana, eh Dr. Phillpott."

04
SECTION ZERO 4 OF FOUR EXPERIMENTAL SECTIONS. THIS SECTION HAS SPAWNED MANY FUSIONS OF THE PREVIOUS EXPERIMENT RESULTING IN THE BIRTH OF A NEW BREED OF VISUAL EXPLOSIONS. YOU HAVE BEEN WARNED.

"Uh? Yes sir. Er, sir? Colour breakdown 43 parts per 100 sir. Rising steadily."

"Do we have enough to continue at this intake?"

"At this intake, yes sir, but like I said, they keep taking more. We don't need to pump it in to them, they're taking it in themselves."

"Hmmm…"

"Sir. Brain activity is reading off the metre. This can't be right. Sir?"

"78 parts per 100. Something very bad is happening."

"Sir, I'm not sure, but I think… I can confirm with a few tests, but I think they're already creating their own fonts sir."

"Logos?"

"No sir, whole fonts. It's…"

"Good lord."

"Should we shut them down?"

"No, no, don't be silly. We're totally safe. No need to worry, just watch.

This is science, boy."

"Sir, ink banks almost drained."

"Backups."

"Backups already on sir. We should shut them down."

"No!"

"Sir. They're hooking into our ISDN lines; all the phone lines… locked up solid. And not just downloading sir. They're sending files out."

"This is incredible…"

"Er. Oh. The cable TV lines too. Sir, I think…"

"…Just incredible."

"Breached security sir. Not just the firewall or the phones either, the lab security has been breached. I think… confirm all units? All units confirmed. Uh. Sir? They're…"

"I know Phillpott… they're gone…"

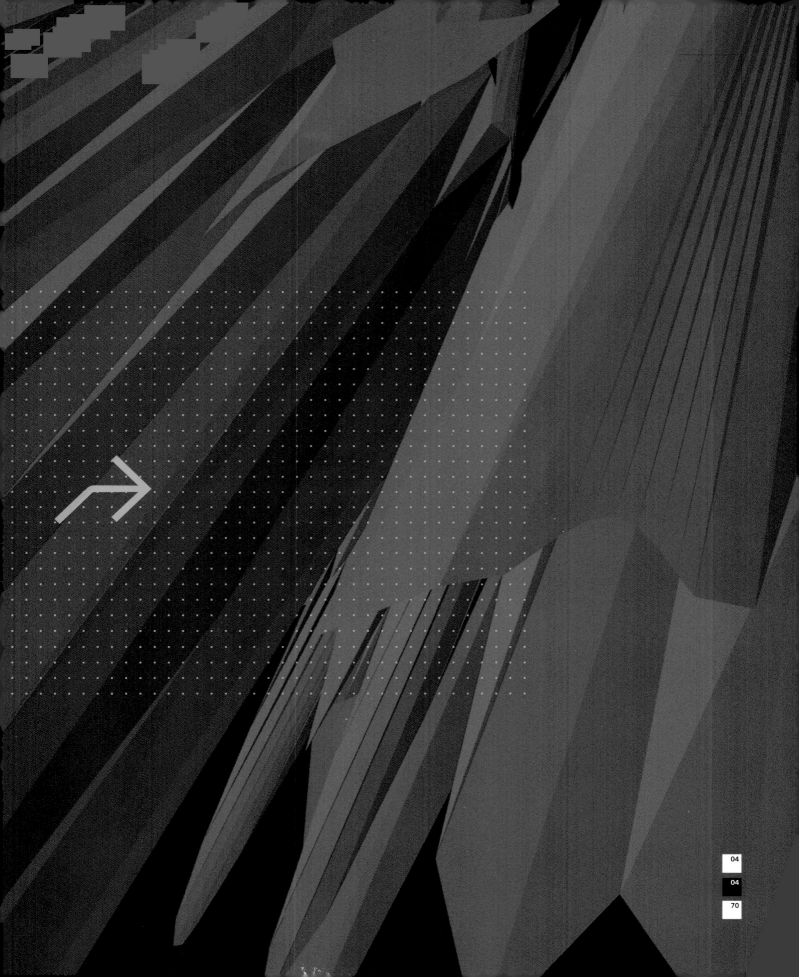

04
04
70

01

04
10
76

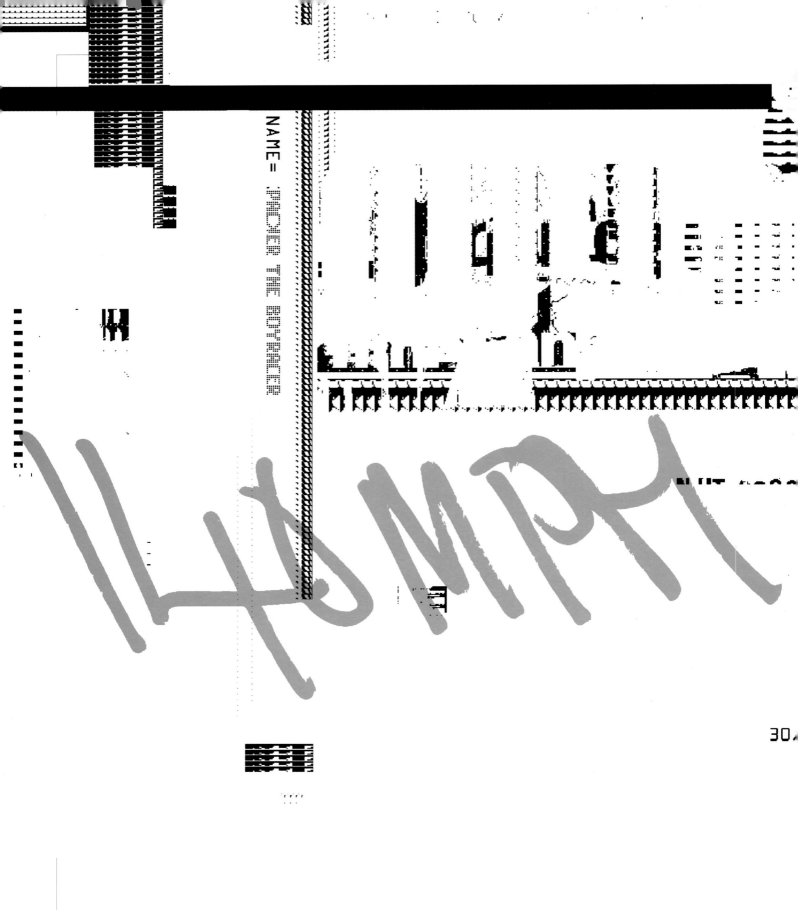

NAME= UNDER THE BOMBER

30

STRIP OF MESSAGE
THE
EXPERIMENT
NEVER
ENDS
END OF MESSAGE

The world as you see it is reality, and everyone has their own reality.

Our personal reality is shaped by everything in our lives. Our DNA, our parents and families, the friends we have, the books we read, the places we go, our height, shoe size, bra size. The movies we watch and the transport we use. The people we've met, loved, fucked, dumped, hated, killed and buried in the desert.

Everyone's reality is particular to them. Of course, we are all human beings, part of this planet, so our different dimensions cross, touch, meet at many places, making it seem like we're all living on the same plane of existence. In reality, each plane is no more than a layer in Photoshop, millions of layers making up the image we call the world. Flatten that image, make everyone the same, and the world would be a far less confusing, but also less interesting, place to live.

This book has been an experiment with print, and an experiment in reality. Take one man's reality, and pass it on. What do you make of it? What can you add? Can the lessons of your reality add to another's? Can they add by subtraction? What if someone were to wipe away your vision of the world and replace it with his or her own. Who makes you? You or your reality? Are we willing to learn from another's vision of The Truth?

This was the purpose of our experiment on this group of people. We remixed their realities, and made them whole. From their minds, through electricity and into your hands. Will they become part of your reality? Maybe they've already asserted their influence; you just don't know it yet? Everyone wants you to see things "their way"; maybe you should just give in. It's time to accept the fact that, though you may disagree with everyone and everything, we are all still "right". Everyone's reality is the truth to them. And this book is a reality that is Fold7.

Can you handle this truth? It's out there. Somewhere. And so is the multi-layered, multi-disciplined, multi-talented laboratory creation known as Fold7.

We have compiled this book, this collection of research and mass experimentation, to prepare you for the time when you too are witness to the blinding light of creation, a light created by the special mix of minds and talents now recognized by the world as one unit, a unit named Fold7. Forewarned is forearmed after all.

So it is with strong hopes for a glorious future that this experiment is concluded. Much has been learnt from those we sought to teach, and, as the search for ultimate knowledge is our life's quest, we will continue to search this world for the escaped subjects of our experimentation. An experiment that has given us a new hope, and a dream that one day our paths will cross Fold7's again.

Professor Charles Anzee. 26th November 2001

The research continues. If you have information concerning the activities of Fold7, please contact Professor Anzee via the experimental website www.fold7.com/chemistry. All sightings of Fold7-produced media should be recorded and catalogued for future research.

We thank you for your co-operation.

Fold7 are

SIMON PACKER
RYAN NEWEY
HENRY OBASI
NICK HAYES
KAT STUBBINGS
MARTIN FEWELL
LEE FASCIANI
JOHN YORKE
ANGELA CROWE
TIM BOLDERSON
SIMON THOMPSON
AND DAVE THE CHIMP

Photographers

Inside back cover · Justin De Deney,
retouching by Fold7
Section 01·14·16 · Guy Baker
Section 03·07·47 · Ryk
Section 03·09·49 · Guy Baker
Section 03·14·54 · Guy Baker
Section 03 pull-out · Mario Godlewski, Guy Baker

www.fold7.com   mail@fold7.com

SPECIAL THANKS TO:
TIMO ARNALL, SALLY COE, MELANIE CO
ALDENHOVEN, LUCAS KRULL (LOOPPO
NAPPER, RICH WALLETT, JAMES MULLE
CREW (DIGITALSTATIC.CO.UK), CHRIST
INDUSTRIES, UCHENNA, OKOCHA, CHINU
KAREN BATCHELOR, PAT SCOVELL, JAME
AND DENNIS, DARYL, MATT COLMAN, T
JULIAN GERMAIN, SCOTT GRAHAM, LIND
GAVIN BULLEN, BRAM, JACQUI MCELRO
NAN, THOMAS NAPPER, DAVE GAULLER,
NIKKI FABLE, BEN HARRISSON, GABRIE
ROBINSON, SUE CLIFFORD, SAM FOREST,
GREG SUTTON, EDDIE SHORT, DOMINIQ
SHAH, EMMA POOLE, KEN, SAM WEBST
OLENA BAKER, HSBC CREDIT CARD, MI
EVANS, RUPERT, HAWAR RAOUF, SEAN
TOTTO, NICK COTTAGE, NICOLA GREEN
CODRINGTON, MARTIN CONWAY, HARRI
DROGMAN, JOHN CARD, MARGRET, OS
GRESHAM, PAUL ARNOLD, FUSED AND B
RICHARD CRABB, HITEN, DAREN COO
JOHNSTON, FIONA, CARLO D'ALANNO,
BARRIE, PAUL, LATISHA, GEORGE CRABB
KELLY, SASHA, LIZA SAVAGE, SOPHIE FLA
SOWMAN, JAT, KARA, CATRIN, MATTHE
ZIMMERMAN, JACKIE WATSON, BEN SPE
HORRIX, ELVINA FLOWER, PAUL HARRO
VESSEY, JOEL LIMA, BENITA, GRAHAM PA

JAKE KNIGHT, CHRIS KENNY, HELEN JONES, MARCUS RESPRINGER, TOBY
ACTORY.COM), ANDREW CASHER, SEAN CLARK, NINA NAGEL, THOMAS
CHAD REA, ED POTTER, ELLIOT WALTERS, OWAIN GEORGE, DIGITAL STATIC
ROTH AND THE 'MOB, ROB DOUGAN, CHIMP FAMILY AND MONKEY
OE, ROJER, MARTHA, TRACEY, DANNY, KEVIN, DAVID BARROW, KEVIN HAYES,
ULSON, DAVID HODGSON, RENIER, JULIA CARTA, NICKIE DUKU, CHRISTINE
DEREK, CRAIG, MATT CROXFORD, EMMA, DUNCAN CHAYNE, DAVE FROST,
TURNHAM, SUZIE, JOEL, EDDIE, JEAN LINDLEY, JAMES HARRIS, MADELINE,
ALEY SAUNDERS, ALEX MCNUTT, CHRIS MEIN, YASMINE, SIMON HAWTREY,
RON HEGARTY, GLEN BROWN, IAN PACKER, JAMES PACKER, PETER PACKER,
JAMES, GRAZIELA PRIESER, KATIE REAGAN, SIMEON RICE, NOEL, RICHARD
RK SARGENT, DAVID BAKER, SARAH SHAW, GWEN, GAVIN, DAVID OSBOURNE,
PLUMLEY, MEREDITH, CONRAD FREETHY, TOM GLANVILLE, MARTIN, KETAN
ALEX (DENTIST), RHIAN ASKINS, MORAG MCINNES, SHEELAGH MATCHET,
'BRIEN, CHARLIE, KEVIN, MUM AND DAD, FLUER, KATE ANCKETILL, PETER
IS, SEAN CLARK, GAVIN, SIM WISHLADE, TYRA SMUDE, DAVID LOVELOCK,
AM CURLEY, JP, DAN MAXTED, CHARLIE PRICE, CHRISTIAN BROGI, GILES
ABIGAIL ARMFIELD, NICK KEEGAN, ANDY MCKAY, STEPHEN ABBOTT, DAN
, URBAN SPACES, JOHN SCRIVENER, RICHARD JOHNSON, GRANT, MATT
SED, JENNY, RUTH BOLTON, JOHN HUNT, BRADLEY, BARRY, SUE MCGREGOR,
ELISSA PARNEL, ROGER HILL, SHRUTI SYNGAL, HAZEL EGNER, ANANT
DSAY, DEBBIE FEIGER, SAFFI, SID, JOHNATHAN BRIGGS, PIP, LISA/DAN
M HILARY, SARAH HUMPHRIES, MYN, ADAM SCOTT, JAZEL, BRIAN HEPPELL,
ER, JASON EDWARDS, ADAM HAYES, LIZ GRAVES, JAN DIRK BOUW, NARGIZA
EY, DAHLAN LASSALLE, ALLIE WEST, SAM PRYOR, YVONNE NASH, JORG
R, JO LIGHTFOOT, FELICITY, STEVE FIRTH, LUCIANA PRIEST, CHEYNE, NICOLA
SABINE GILLERT, LUCY WILSDON, MARK HANEY, MARK LAUGHLAN, JOHN
ER, PAULA AND LINDA, CHRIS FROST, AND ERICA.

FOLD 7 WANT YOUR CHILDREN

New studies of the effects of evil on brain chemistry help to explain why many people, creative-types in particular, experience long-lasting feelings of pleasure and release through being "bad". Evil makes happy designers.

Results from animal studies, and more importantly studies of children, have revealed that just five minutes of un-godly thoughts can release large quantities of the brain's supplies of dopamine, gamma aminobutyric acid, opioid peptides and serotonin systems - chemicals responsible for our feelings of pleasure and well-being.

Be bad - feel good. Work for Us